ALL ABOUT JESUS ACTIVITY BOOK

written by

ANITA REITH STOHS

illustrated by

CORBIN HILLAM

CPH
SAINT LOUIS

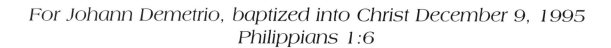

For Johann Demetrio, baptized into Christ December 9, 1995
Philippians 1:6

Copyright © 1997 Concordia Publishing House
3558 S. Jefferson Avenue, St. Louis, MO 63118-3968
Manufactured in the United States of America

1   2   3   4   5   6   7   8   9   10   06   05   04   03   02   01   00   99   98   97

An Angel Appears to Mary

The angel Gabriel told Mary that she would be the mother of God's Son. Gabriel told Mary to name her baby Jesus. Jesus came to earth to be our Savior. Make an angel ornament.

What to Do

Ask an adult to photocopy this page, or you can trace the angel shapes on paper. Cut out the shapes. Fold them in half. Stand the angels so the folded edges touch. Glue the wings that are back to back together to make a 3-D angel. Punch a hole at the top and tie a piece of yarn through it. Hang the angel on your Christmas tree.

Now Try This

Trace the shapes on different kinds of paper. Follow the steps to make more angels. You could make a whole chorus!

Look for angels in other activities.

GLUE

Jesus Is Born

A manger is a feeding box for animals.

Joseph and Mary traveled to Bethlehem because the government was taking a census. When they arrived, they didn't have a place to stay. Mary and Joseph had to sleep in a stable. While they were there, Jesus was born. Mary wrapped Him in soft cloths and laid Him in a manger. Make this Christmas decoration that shows Jesus lying in His manger bed.

What to Do

Ask an adult to photocopy this page. Use the code to color the picture. Cut out the circle. Punch a hole at the top and tie a piece of yarn through it. Display your work.

Code
- • = Yellow
- •• = Brown
- ••• = Blue

Shepherds Hear about Jesus

"The Savior is born," an angel told the shepherds. Then angels filled the night sky and sang praises to God. Connect the dots to finish the picture. Make up your own song to praise God for sending Jesus to be your Savior.

The Shepherds Visit Jesus

After the angels left, the shepherds ran to Bethlehem to see baby Jesus. When they found Him, they worshiped Him. Then the shepherds left and told everyone they met about the Baby sent to be our Savior.

What to Do

Ask an adult to photocopy this page. Color the puppets. Cut them out. Glue the ends of each strip of paper together to make a tube. Use these finger puppets to act out the story of the angel's message and the shepherds' response.

Now Try This

Cover a shoe box with construction paper. Use stickers, marking pens, or crayons to decorate the box. Use the box as the stable and put your finger puppets inside to make your own manger set.

Tell someone the story of Jesus' birth.

The Wise Men Visit Jesus

Wise Men from the East followed the star to find a child who was born to be king. The star led them to the house where Mary, Joseph, and the child Jesus were living. When the Wise Men found Jesus, they worshiped Him. We worship Jesus because He is our King. Help the Wise Men find their way to Jesus.

God Protects Jesus in Egypt

After the Wise Men left, God sent an angel to tell Joseph that Jesus was in danger. The angel said to take Mary and Jesus to Egypt to escape wicked King Herod who wanted to kill Jesus. After King Herod died, God told Joseph to take Jesus and Mary home. The family returned to Nazareth. Help Joseph find the right path to Nazareth.

The Boy Jesus Visits Jerusalem

When Jesus was 12 years old, He took a special trip with Joseph and Mary. Put the underlined words in the story into the crossword puzzle. Some letters have been given as clues.

When Jesus was TWELVE years old, He went to JERUSALEM with Mary and Joseph. They went to the city to celebrate the PASSOVER. After the celebration, MARY and JOSEPH started back to Nazareth. After traveling for a day, they couldn't find JESUS. They returned to Jerusalem and SEARCHED everywhere for Him. Finally, they went to the TEMPLE. They found Jesus talking with the TEACHERS. Jesus told Mary she should have known He would be in His Father's HOUSE. Who was Jesus' real Father?

What would you talk with Jesus about if He came to your church?

Jesus' Baptism

When Jesus was baptized by His cousin John, God's Holy Spirit came down in the form of a dove. A voice from heaven spoke. God said, "You are My Son, whom I love; with You I am well pleased."

What to Do

Ask an adult to photocopy this page. Write your name and your Baptism date on the lines below the dove. Color the frame yellow. Use different bright crayons to color the spaces with dots. Cut out the picture. Punch a hole at the top and tie a piece of yarn through it. Dip a cotton ball in cooking oil and rub it across the whole picture. Hang your stained-glass picture in a sunny window.

"I Was Baptized" by Arnold C. Mueller. Text from *A Child's Garden of Song*. Copyright © 1949 Concordia Publishing House.

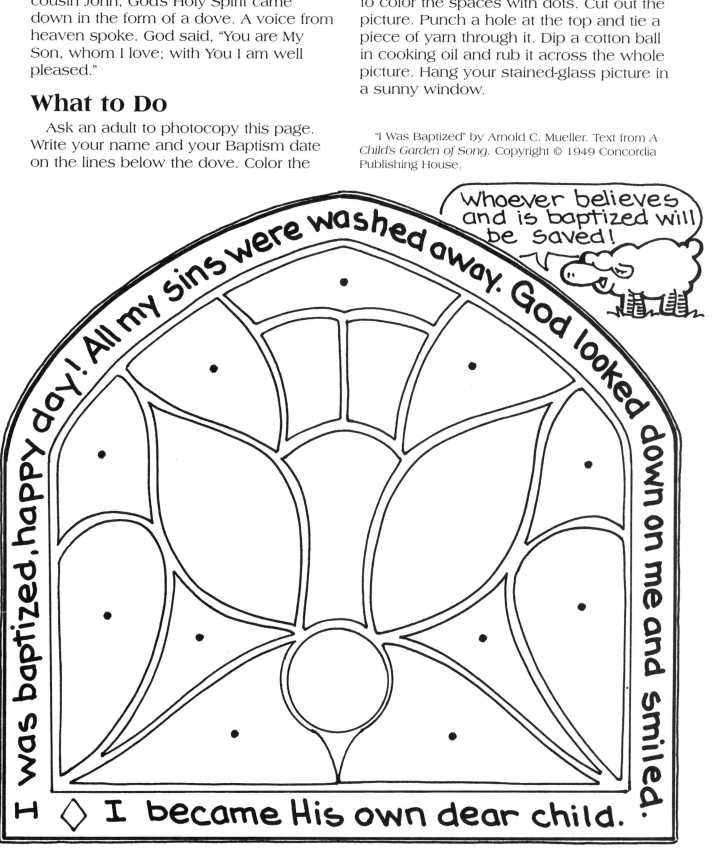

Jesus' First Miracle

What was the first miracle Jesus did? Use a dark crayon to color in these spaces in the jug: 1, 3, 4, 6, 7, 8, 9, 11, 12, 13, 14, 16, 17, 19, and 20. Read the words in the spaces that aren't colored to find Jesus' first miracle.

Jesus can do anything.

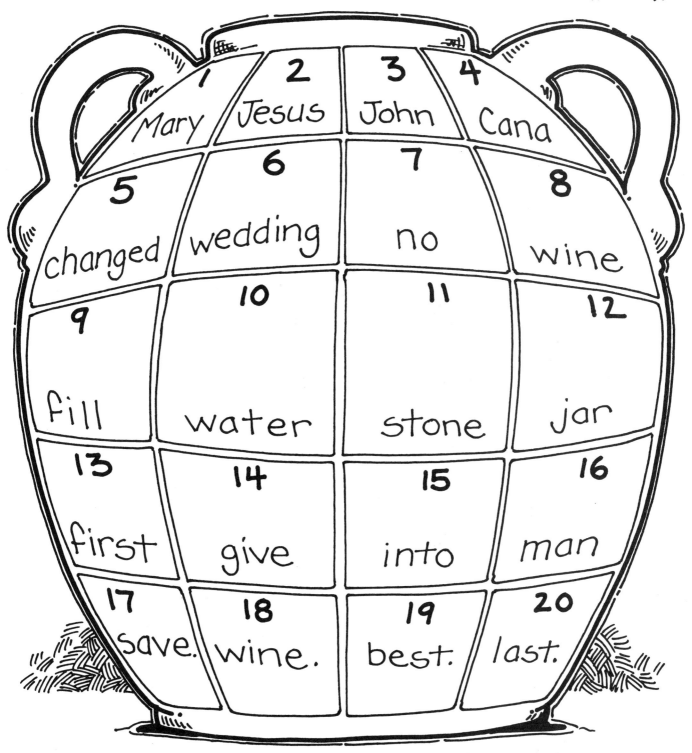

1 Mary	2 Jesus	3 John	4 Cana
5 changed	6 wedding	7 no	8 wine
9 fill	10 water	11 stone	12 jar
13 first	14 give	15 into	16 man
17 save.	18 wine.	19 best.	20 last.

Jesus Calls His Disciples

As Jesus walked by the Sea of Galilee one day, He called four fishermen to follow Him. "I will make you fishers of men," Jesus told them. Jesus has called you to follow Him too. He will help you tell others about His great love. Make a "fishers-of-people" mobile to remind you of Jesus' call.

What to Do

Ask an adult to photocopy this page, or you can trace the shapes on paper and write the words yourself. Color the boat and fish. Cut them out. Lay the pieces in a column to read: Jesus says, Be Fishers of People. Turn the shapes over. Lay a piece of yarn down the middle of the shapes but leave a long tail above the boat. Tape the yarn to each shape. Tie a loop in the yarn above the boat. Display the mobile.

Jesus Talks with Nicodemus

"For God so loved the world," Jesus told a man named Nicodemus, "that He gave His one and only Son, that whoever believes in Him shall not perish but have eternal life." God loved us so much that He sent Jesus to die for our sins. Because Jesus died and rose again, our sins are forgiven and we'll live in heaven with Him forever.

What to Do

Use the code below to color in the spaces in the circle. Then you'll see a symbol that shows how much Jesus loves you.

Code

Blue: 1 and 9

Green: 3 and 7

Brown: 2, 4, 5, 6, and 8

Red: 10

God loves you too!

1   2   3

5

4   10   6

7   8   9

Jesus Heals a Little Boy

"Come home with me and help my son," a man asked Jesus. "He is dying."

Jesus didn't go to the man's house. Instead, He said, "Go home. Your son will live."

The man left. His servants met him as he traveled home. They told the man his son was better. The man asked, "When did he get better?" Use the code to solve the puzzle and learn when the boy was healed.

Jesus Helps Us Follow Him

"Follow Me," Jesus said to His 12 friends. "Follow Me," Jesus says to you. But you can't follow Jesus on your own. That's why Jesus has promised to help us follow His footsteps. Make a footprint poster to remind you that Jesus walks with you.

What to Do

Ask an adult to photocopy this page. Trace your shoe on the left side of the poster. Write your name on the line on the right side. Color the poster. Cut it out. (If your shoe is too big for the paper, draw it on a larger sheet of paper. Then tape the paper to the section with Jesus on it.)

FOLLOWS JESUS

Jesus Shows His Friends How to Pray

"Teach us to pray," Jesus' friends asked.

Do you know the prayer Jesus taught His friends? It begins "Our Father in heaven." Jesus told us we could talk to our heavenly Father anytime, about anything.

What to Do

Ask an adult to photocopy this page. Color the border around the Lord's Prayer. Add your own pictures to the border. Cut out the picture and hang it as a reminder to pray to God every day.

Now Try This

Glue the picture to a sheet of construction paper. Punch holes around the sides. Lace yarn through the holes.

Pray the Lord's Prayer today.

Our Father who art in heaven,
hallowed be Thy name,
Thy kingdom come,
Thy will be done
on earth as in heaven.
Give us this day our daily bread;
and forgive us our trespasses
as we forgive those
who trespass against us;
and lead us not into temptation,
but deliver us from evil.
For Thine is the kingdom
and the power and the glory
forever and ever. Amen.

Jesus Teaches about God's Love

"God cares for the flowers," Jesus told everyone who was listening to Him teach. "Because He takes care of something so little, He must take very good care of you!" We know God takes special care of us. He sent Jesus to take care of our biggest problem—sin. Jesus won forgiveness for us on the cross.

What to Do

Match the number and letter in the small square to the number and letter of the large square. Then copy the shapes or lines into the large square. When you finish, you'll see something beautiful that God created. The first square has been done for you.

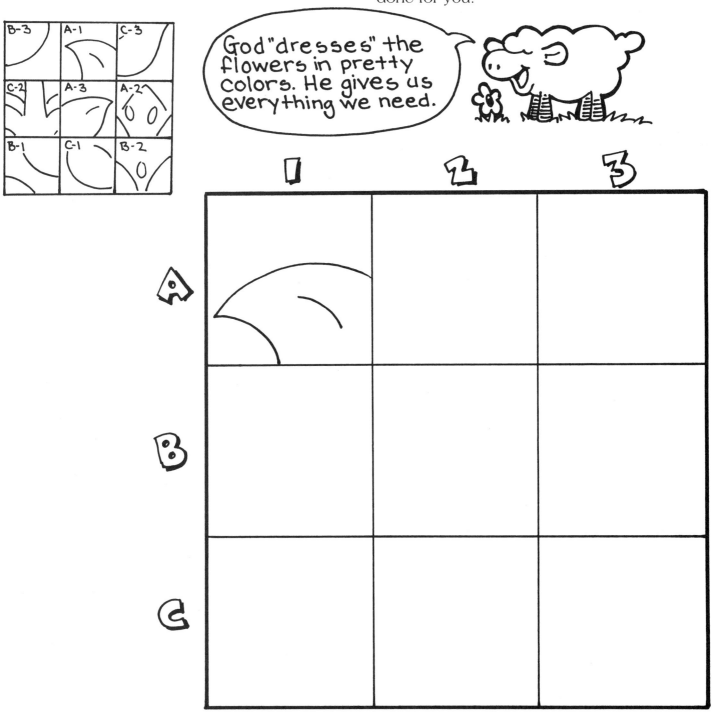

Jesus, Our Good Shepherd

Jesus told a story about a shepherd who had 100 sheep. One day, one sheep got lost. The shepherd looked and looked for the lost sheep. When he found it, he was very happy. He picked up the sheep and carried it home.

Jesus is your Good Shepherd. He found you when you were lost and alone. He leads you on the path to heaven.

What to Do

Ask an adult to photocopy this page, or trace the shepherd and sheep on paper. Color the figures. Cut them out. Glue a craft stick to the back of each figure to make puppets. Use them to tell someone the story of the lost sheep.

Now Try This

Glue cotton balls on the sheep. Use scraps of wallpaper or construction paper to make "clothes" for the shepherd.

The Prodigal Son

Jesus told a story about a man with two sons. The younger son asked for his part of his father's money. Then he left home. He wasted the money on fancy things and fun times. He used up all of it. He had to take a job feeding pigs, but he still didn't have enough money to buy food. The son went back home. He asked his father to forgive him for being selfish and running away. His father was very happy to have his son back. He forgave the boy.

Who forgives our sins and takes us back into His family? Connect the dots to find the answer.

Jesus Calms the Storm

A big wind made the waves hit hard against the boat. Jesus' friends were scared. They woke up Jesus. "Save us!" they cried. What did Jesus do? Each box with a letter is connected to an empty box by a line. Follow the lines and write the letter in the empty boxes to find out what Jesus said.

L T L E S B I

AND IT WAS

Jesus is stronger than any storm.

Jesus Brings a Girl Back to Life

"The little girl is dead," the people told Jesus as He came to the girl's home. What happened next? Write the first letter of each picture on the line above the picture to find the answer.

How do you think the girl felt when she woke up and saw Jesus?

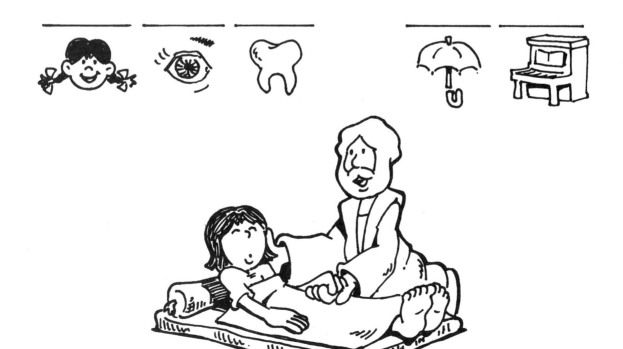

Jesus Feeds 5,000 People

The people listened to Jesus talk all day. It was time for supper. But there weren't any stores or restaurants for the people to get food. Everyone was hungry. Jesus used two fish and five loaves of bread from a little boy's lunch to feed more than 5,000 people. Before He fed the people, Jesus thanked God for the food.

What to Do

Draw a picture of your favorite food in the upper right corner of the plate. Then write God a thank-You prayer for it.

Jesus Heals 10 Men

Jesus healed 10 men who were sick with leprosy. The men ran to show the priests they were healed. Only one man came back to say thank You to Jesus. Help the thankful man get through the maze to thank Jesus.

Remember to thank God for all the good things He does for you.

Jesus Blesses the Children

"Go away!" Jesus' friends said to the mothers and their children.

"Let the children come," said Jesus. He picked them up, touched them, and blessed them.

What to Do

Draw faces and hair on the faces around Jesus. Maybe you could make the faces look like your friends or your family members. Draw your face in the space below Jesus' face.

Jesus Meets Zacchaeus

Zacchaeus was a little man. He climbed up in a tree to see Jesus. When Jesus walked by, He looked up in the tree. "Come down, Zacchaeus," Jesus said. "I'm going to your house today."

What to Do

Find Zacchaeus in the tree. List the other things that are hidden in the tree.

Jesus Enters Jerusalem

Jesus sent two of His disciples to find a donkey. He planned to ride into Jerusalem on the animal. The disciples found the donkey right where Jesus said it would be. As Jesus rode into Jerusalem, the people threw palm branches and coats on the road. They shouted "Hosanna" and sang songs of praise to God.

What to Do

Can you find the donkey in this picture? Color the areas with the letter *B* black and the areas with the letter *G* gray.

Jesus Gives His Disciples a New Meal

The night that Jesus was betrayed, He took bread and wine and gave it to His disciples. "This is My body. This is My blood," Jesus said. "Do this in remembrance of Me." We still celebrate this meal. We call it Holy Communion or the Lord's Supper.

What to Do

Connect the dots to draw two symbols for the Holy Supper Jesus started that night.

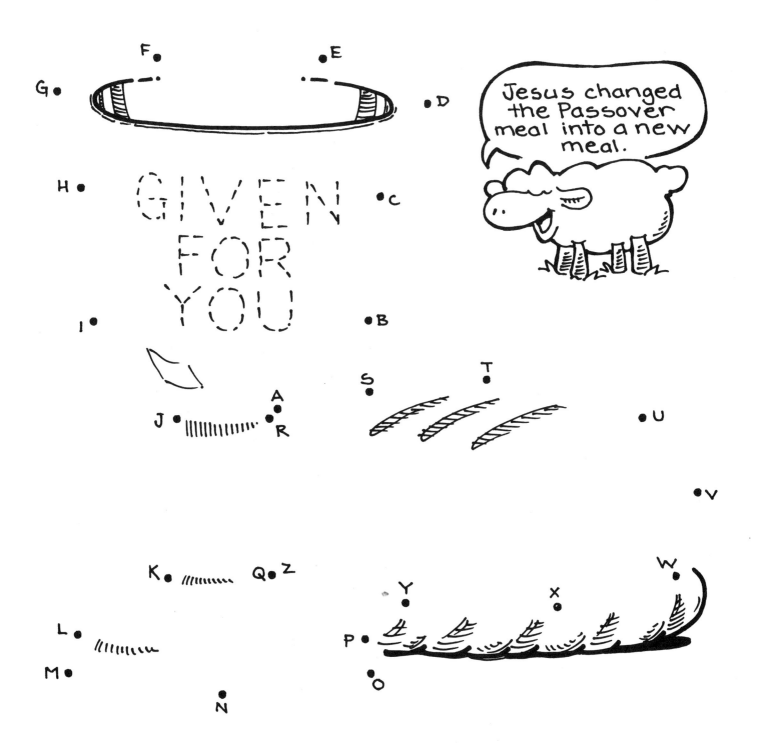

Jesus' Death

Jesus died on the cross for our sins. It was very sad that Jesus died, but His death defeated the devil and sin. God worked something very good from Jesus' death. That's why we call the day He died Good Friday. But Jesus did not stay dead. He came back to life again on the first Easter morning.

What to Do
Work each subtraction problem. Then connect the dots to finish the picture.

Now Try This
Use crayons or marking pens to change this Good Friday cross into a happy Easter one. You might add flowers and butterflies or use bright colors to make a rainbow cross.

9-3=

9-2=

8-4=   7-2=

10-2=   12-3=

6-3=   4-2=

12-1=   11-1=

Jesus died to win us forgiveness.

2-1=   START

12-0=

Jesus Comes Back to Life

Three women went to the tomb early on the first Easter. "Who will roll away the stone for us?" they asked one another. When they got to the tomb, the stone was rolled away. An angel was inside the tomb. "Jesus is risen!" the angel told the women. What wonderful news! Help the women find the path to the tomb.

Jesus Appears to Thomas

Thomas did not believe that Jesus was alive. He wasn't in the room when Jesus appeared to the other disciples. But Thomas was in the room the next time Jesus appeared. What did Thomas say to Jesus?

What to Do

Use the code to complete the words Thomas said. The first word has been done for you.

Jesus Returns to Heaven

The time came for Jesus to go back to heaven. He took His friends and His disciples to a hill. Then He said good-bye and rose up in the sky until a cloud hid Him from sight. Two angels came and told the disciples Jesus would return just like He had left.

Even though we can't see Jesus, we know He's with us. He sent His Spirit to live within us.

What to Do

Connect the dots to complete the picture of Jesus. Draw yourself next to Him.

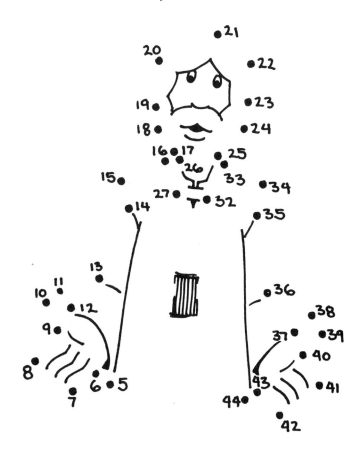

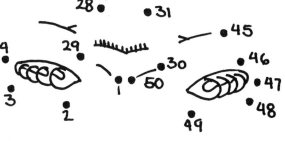

Someday we will live with Jesus in heaven.

Jesus Gave Us His Word

Jesus doesn't live on earth anymore. We can't listen to Him teach or preach. We can't watch Him do miracles. But we do have a wonderful book that tells us all about Jesus. We can read about Jesus every day in the Bible. And when we read about Jesus, God's Holy Spirit makes our faith stronger.

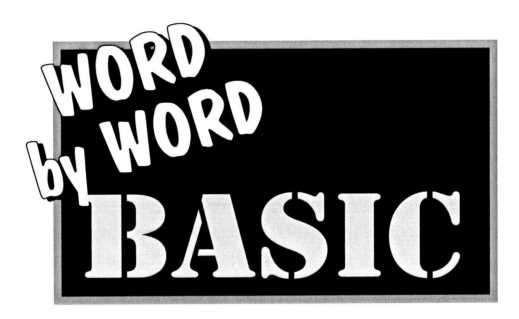

LITERACY TEST PACKAGE

Midterm   (Basic Picture Dictionary pages 1–85)
Final   (Basic Picture Dictionary pages 86–165)

Steven J. Molinsky · Bill Bliss

Contributing Author
Ann Kennedy

PRENTICE HALL REGENTS
A Pearson Education Company
White Plains, NY 10606-1951

Editorial Director: *Allen Ascher*
Director of Design and Production: *Rhea Banker*
Associate Director of Electronic Publishing: *Aliza Greenblatt*
Electronic Production Editor: *Wendy Wolf*
Senior Manufacturing Manager: *Patrice Fraccio*
Manufacturing Buyer: *Dave Dickey*
Cover Designer: *Merle Krumper*
Pre-formatter: *Rose Ann Merrey*
Production Manager: *Ray Keating*

Illustrated by RICHARD E. HILL

The authors gratefully acknowledge the contribution of Tina Carver
in the development of the *Word by Word* program.

Printed in the United States of America

10   9   8   7   6   5   4   3   2   1

ISBN 0-13-624677-X

Prentice-Hall International (UK) Limited, *London*
Prentice-Hall of Australia Pty. Limited, *Sydney*
Prentice-Hall Canada Inc., *Toronto*
Prentice-Hall Hispanoamericana, S. A., *Mexico*
Prentice-Hall of India Private Limited, *New Delhi*
Prentice-Hall of Japan, Inc., *Tokyo*
Prentice-Hall Asia, *Singapore*
Editora Prentice-Hall do Brasil, Ltda., *Rio de Janeiro*

CHOOSE THE CORRECT WORD

1. house
   apartment

2. cucumber
   carrot

3. eggs
   grapes

4. class
   glass

5. bed
   deck

6. refrigerator
   dishwasher

7. pillow
   window

8. soda
   sofa

9. hamper
   hammer

10. cookies
    cookbook

11. television
    toaster

12. drain
    chair

MATCHING

<table>
<tr><td>**1.** NIECE</td><td>grill</td></tr>
<tr><td>**2.** KNIFE</td><td>bank</td></tr>
<tr><td>**3.** BANK</td><td>freezer</td></tr>
<tr><td>**4.** FREEZER</td><td>knife</td></tr>
<tr><td>**5.** GRILL</td><td>niece</td></tr>
</table>

WHAT'S THE WORD?

| board | book | desk | pencil | student | teacher |

1. _____   4. _____

2. _____   5. _____

3. _____   6. _____

WRITE YOUR PERSONAL INFORMATION

1. Name: _____
   FIRST   LAST

2. Address: _____
   NUMBER   STREET   APT.

3. _____
   CITY   STATE   ZIP CODE

4. Telephone Number: _____

MATCHING: NUMBERS

1. fifth		1st
2. one half		1/4
3. first		2nd
4. seventy-five percent		3rd
5. second		5th
6. one fourth		11th
7. eleventh		1/2
8. third		75%

WHAT DO YOU DO EVERY DAY?

comb	do	eat	get up	sleep	study

1. I _____ dinner. 2. I _____ my hair. 3. I _____.

4. I _____. 5. I _____. 6. I _____ the laundry.

CHOOSE THE CORRECT ANSWER

1. a. I brush my hair.
   b. I brush my teeth.

2. a. I take a shower.
   b. I take a bath.

3. a. He's my son.
   b. She's my daughter.

4. a. They're my grandchildren.
   b. They're my grandparents.

CHOOSE THE CORRECT WORD

1. painter
   answer

2. dresser
   gardener

3. creamer
   electrician

4. plumber
   number

5. doorbell
   locksmith

6. carpenter
   trailer

MATCHING

1. 2 x 5 = 10

   Six divided by three equals two.

2. 6 ÷ 3 = 2

   Thirteen minus one equals twelve.

3.
   $$\begin{array}{r} 7 \\ +\ 2 \\ \hline 9 \end{array}$$

   Two times five equals ten.

4.
   $$\begin{array}{r} 13 \\ -\ 1 \\ \hline 12 \end{array}$$

   Seven plus two equals nine.

CHOOSE THE CORRECT ANSWER

1. a. Raise your hand.
   b. Erase the mistake.

2. a. Wash the dishes.
   b. Watch a movie.

3. a. Close your book.
   b. Sit down.

4. a. Lower the shades.
   b. Turn off the lights.

5. a. Correct the mistakes.
   b. Collect the tests.

6. a. Go to the board.
   b. Work in groups.

7. a. Read page eight.
   b. Check your answers.

8. a. Answer the questions.
   b. Hand in your homework.

CHOOSE THE CORRECT TIME

1. two fifteen
   three ten

2. six twenty
   half past four

3. a quarter to seven
   a quarter after seven

WHAT'S MISSING?

December   September   June   March   Friday   Tuesday

1. April, May, _____

2. Sunday, Monday, _____

3. January, February, _____

4. October, November, _____

5. Wednesday, Thursday, _____

6. July, August, _____

CHOOSE THE CORRECT PLACE

1. classroom
   bus station

2. gas station
   hardware store

3. drug store
   bookstore

4. clinic
   cleaners

5. library
   laundromat

6. supermarket
   superintendent

MATCHING: OPPOSITES

1. hot   small

2. tall   young

3. old   full

4. slow   bad

5. large   cold

6. good   fast

7. easy   short

8. empty   difficult

CHOOSE THE CORRECT WORD

1. dry
wet

2. messy
neat

3. sad
surprised

4. happy
sick

5. mushroom
onion

6. corn
crackers

MATCHING

1. orange   seat

2. fire   beef

3. dental   juice

4. car   floss

5. shopping   alarm

6. baby   milk

7. ground   mall

8. chocolate   powder

CHOOSE THE CORRECT WORD

1. table
   tablet

2. track
   stamp

3. milk
   brick

4. weather
   sweater

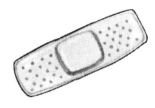

5. bandaid
   band

6. sew
   saw

7. suit
   suitcase

8. mailbox
   booth

9. shirt
   skirt

10. ladder
    lumber

11. mask
    math

12. cough
    coffee

MATCHING

1.	hat	wrist
2.	shoes	eyes
3.	watch	head
4.	ring	hands
5.	gloves	waist
6.	scarf	finger
7.	sunglasses	neck
8.	belt	feet

MATCHING

1.	eat	a magazine
2.	drink	a truck
3.	read	a taco
4.	play	jeans
5.	drive	lemonade
6.	wear	soccer

CHOOSE THE CORRECT WORD

1. stock clerk
   cashier

2. bicycling
   baseball

3. subway
   meter

4. waitress
   waiter

5. a bag of flour
   a box of crackers

6. dentist
   delivery person

7. cookbook
   chef

8. swimming
   skiing

9. janitor
   jogging

10. briefcase
    bricklayer

11. a dozen eggs
    a container of
    blueberries

12. coach
    accelerator

WHAT'S THE AMOUNT?

I.   thirty cents

2.    one cent

3.   twenty-five cents

4.   five cents

5.   five dollars

MATCHING: OPPOSITES

I. fancy   short

2. heavy   low

3. high   plain

4. wide   tight

5. long   light

6. loose   narrow

CHOOSE THE CORRECT ANSWER

1. a. It's clear.
   b. It's cloudy.

2. a. It's winter.
   b. It's summer.

3. a. It's a hurricane.
   b. It's foggy.

4. a. I have the chills.
   b. I have a headache.

5. a. I'm going to sneeze.
   b. I'm going to sprain.

6. a. I hurt my arm.
   b. I hurt my leg.

7. a. It's a beautiful vest.
   b. It's a green dress.

8. a. Peel the orange.
   b. Stir the orange.

9. a. It's a bar of soap.
   b. It's a can of soup.

MATCHING

1. shopping   syrup

2. bank   plate

3. cough   book

4. letter   clock

5. time   cart

6. license   carrier

MATCHING

1. seat   desk

2. windshield   ring

3. checkout   belt

4. emergency   guard

5. security   brake

6. key   wipers

WHAT'S THE WORD?

backpack	basketball	football	health	letter	orchestra
package	sandwich	science	shelves	ticket	umbrella

1. _____

2. _____

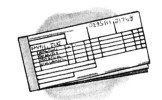

3. _____

4. _____

5. _____

6. _____

7. _____

8. _____

9. _____

10. _____

11. _____

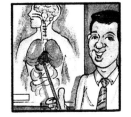

12. _____

MATCHING

1. mechanic   library

2. dishwasher   factory

3. librarian   hospital

4. shopper   service station

5. doctor   supermarket

6. assembler   restaurant

MATCHING

1. postal clerk   office

2. teller   cab

3. secretary   post office

4. barber   airport

5. taxi driver   bank

6. ticket agent   barber shop

MATCHING

1. mow   buildings

2. guard   the piano

3. assemble   lawns

4. play   vegetables

5. scramble   components

6. grow   eggs

CHOOSE THE CORRECT WORD

1. house
2. carrot
3. grapes
4. glass
5. bed
6. refrigerator
7. window
8. soda
9. hammer
10. cookies
11. television
12. chair

MATCHING

1. niece
2. knife
3. bank
4. freezer
5. grill

WHAT'S THE WORD?

1. teacher
2. book
3. pencil
4. desk
5. student
6. board

WRITE YOUR PERSONAL INFORMATION

(Answers will vary)

MATCHING: NUMBERS

1. 5th
2. 1/2
3. 1st
4. 75%
5. 2nd
6. 1/4
7. 11th
8. 3rd

WHAT DO YOU DO EVERY DAY?

1. eat
2. comb
3. get up
4. sleep
5. study
6. do

CHOOSE THE CORRECT ANSWER

1. a
2. b
3. a
4. b

CHOOSE THE CORRECT WORD

1. painter
2. gardener
3. electrician
4. plumber
5. locksmith
6. carpenter

MATCHING

1. Two times five equals ten.
2. Six divided by three equals two.
3. Seven plus two equals nine.
4. Thirteen minus one equals twelve.

CHOOSE THE CORRECT ANSWER

1. a
2. a
3. b
4. a
5. a
6. b
7. b
8. a

CHOOSE THE CORRECT TIME

1. two fifteen
2. half past four
3. a quarter to seven

WHAT'S MISSING?

1. June
2. Tuesday
3. March
4. December
5. Friday
6. September

CHOOSE THE CORRECT PLACE

1. bus station
2. gas station
3. drug store
4. clinic
5. laundromat
6. supermarket

MATCHING: OPPOSITES

1. cold
2. short
3. young
4. fast
5. small
6. bad
7. difficult
8. full

CHOOSE THE CORRECT WORD

1. wet
2. neat
3. sad
4. happy
5. onion
6. corn

MATCHING

1. juice
2. alarm
3. floss
4. seat
5. mall
6. powder
7. beef
8. milk

CHOOSE THE CORRECT WORD

1. table
2. stamp
3. milk
4. sweater
5. bandaid
6. saw
7. suitcase
8. mailbox
9. shirt
10. ladder
11. math
12. cough

MATCHING

1. head
2. feet
3. wrist
4. finger
5. hands
6. neck
7. eyes
8. waist

MATCHING

1. a taco
2. lemonade
3. a magazine
4. soccer
5. a truck
6. jeans

CHOOSE THE CORRECT WORD

1. cashier
2. baseball
3. subway
4. waiter
5. a bag of flour
6. dentist
7. chef
8. swimming
9. jogging
10. bricklayer
11. a dozen eggs
12. coach

WHAT'S THE AMOUNT?

1. twenty-five cents
2. five dollars
3. five cents
4. one cent
5. thirty cents

MATCHING: OPPOSITES

1. plain
2. light
3. low
4. narrow
5. short
6. tight

CHOOSE THE CORRECT ANSWER

1. a
2. b
3. a
4. b
5. a
6. b
7. b
8. a
9. a

MATCHING

1. cart
2. book
3. syrup
4. carrier
5. clock
6. plate

MATCHING

1. belt
2. wipers
3. desk
4. brake
5. guard
6. ring

WHAT'S THE WORD?

1. letter
2. football
3. ticket
4. shelves
5. basketball
6. orchestra
7. sandwich
8. umbrella
9. backpack
10. package
11. science
12. health

MATCHING

1. service station
2. restaurant
3. library
4. supermarket
5. hospital
6. factory

MATCHING

1. post office
2. bank
3. office
4. barber shop
5. cab
6. airport

MATCHING

1. lawns
2. buildings
3. components
4. the piano
5. eggs
6. vegetables